ENGLAND'S LOST LAKE
THE STORY OF WHITTLESEA MERE

Aerial photograph of the bed of Whittlesea Mere. Note the lighter mineral soils of the mere bed, denoting the area of former open water, contrasting with the bordering black peat. Holme Lode Farm in the centre foreground, the birch woodland of Holme Fen Nature Reserve to right.

England's Lost Lake

First Published in 2018 by FastPrint Publishing
Peterborough, England.

A CIP catalogue record for this book is available from the British Library

Paperback ISBN 978-178456-607-4

Printed and bound in England by
www.printondemand-worldwide.com

www.fast-print.net/bookshop

ENGLAND'S LOST LAKE

THE STORY OF WHITTLESEA MERE

Paul Middleton

FastPrint
Publishing

*Dedicated to Eric and Josie
and Margaret
Fenlanders who shared so much
with an Uplander*

List of original contributors

Bernard Chambers, Dennis Clarke, Eric Day, Jayn Gilbert, Margaret Long,
Simon Martin, Kathleen Peach, Alan Swift, Lesley Swift

Contents

Acknowledgements 1

Preface to the First Edition 2

Introduction 4

Origins and Natural History 5

Mere Living 14

Mere Leisure 25

Draining the Mere 32

After the Mere 40

The Great Fen Project 47

References 55

Appendix A: Notes on the flora of Whittleseas Mere area 57

Appendix B: Butterflies and Moths 61

Further reading 65

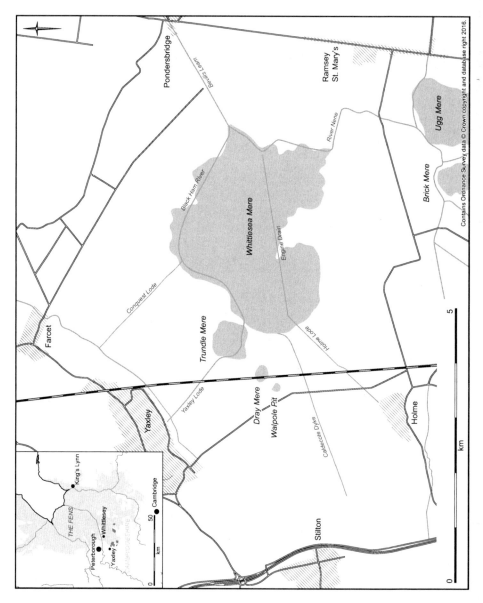

Indicative map to show major features (drawn by Vicki Herring)

Acknowledgements

The idea for re-printing this study of Whittlesea Mere, first published in 1987, came about from a serendipitous meeting between myself and Stewart Howe, to whom much of the credit for its appearance belongs. I am also indebted to Sally Howell for her patience and expertise in producing a succession of amended texts. Our shared enthusiasm for the subject has fuelled our conviction that the story was important enough to re-tell for a generation which now has the opportunity to experience the environmental, social and educational benefits of one of the country's most important re-wilding projects – the Great Fen Project.

The original publication was produced with the support of the WEA Eastern District and I am particularly grateful to them for the readiness with which they gave permission for me to work on the booklet for re-publication.

This also gives me an opportunity to record my grateful thanks to all those who generously gave of their time and experience in face to face interviews during the period of the research for the first publication, and whose stories have provided valuable material for the new chapter "After the Mere". I would also like to record my thanks to Russell Wright for recent helpful conversations.

I hope that the appearance of this revised version of the original booklet will bring much pleasure to any who visit the area with a desire to know more about its history, and will perhaps stimulate and further an interest in this beautiful part of the fens and, in particular, Whittlesea Mere – one of the wonders of Huntingdonshire!

Paul Middleton 2018

Preface to the first edition

This booklet is the outcome of a Workers' Educational Association course on 'The Fens Past and Present', which took place at Whittlesey in spring 1985. The idea for the booklet arose from the desire of students to know more than was already in print about Whittlesea Mere, and from the belief that much unpublished material was available locally to make such a study worthwhile. A short course entitled 'Whittlesea Mere' was held in autumn 1985 to explore the potential of the sources, and eight students from that course, plus one who joined later, volunteered to do the research which has made this booklet possible.

Our study does not claim to be exhaustive. We have concentrated on sources which were readily available to local people who came to the subject with little or no previous experience of historical research. Anyone desiring to further our study would certainly wish to consult the monastic records, the rediscovered Yaxley Lordship archive, and the Fielden estate archive more thoroughly than has been possible in this short study. Nevertheless, we hope to have made a small contribution to the growing literature of local fenland studies firmly grounded in original research. Above all, we hope that our booklet will be found to be both informative and enjoyable.

The project would not have been possible without the sponsorship of the WEA Whittlesey Branch and the WEA Cambridgeshire Federation. Our grateful thanks are also due to the staff of the Huntingdon Record Office, to Dr. Maurice Massey (Nature Conservancy Council East

Midland Region) and the Peterborough Central Reference Library for their guidance and encouragement throughout the project. A number of people made valuable comments on the manuscript, though any errors are our own. Finally, we would wish to thank Mr. John Montague for permission to publish the manuscript letter, printed here for the first time, on page 17 [this edition on page 29].

Paul Middleton, WEA Tutor Organiser for Cambridgeshire

Introduction

"Yaxley Stone Mill,
Glatton Round Hill
and Whittlesey Mere
Are the three great wonders of Huntingdonshire"

The Fens have always held the power to excite and amaze the newcomer. There is a quality in the landscape and the people which marks it out as startlingly different. For the casual observer the enduring impression may be one of unending flatness, straight rivers and prairie fields, whilst the people may seem taciturn, private and severely practical in their view of life. But for the 'uplander' who can give time and ear and eye, there is an unimagined richness and variety and the people, on listening to them and hearing their stories, are warm and full of wisdom. This book is about one small part of the fen, celebrated in its day as a marvel and sought out by travellers from all over the country.

Whittlesea Mere first appears in history in the Anglo-Saxon Chronicle, under the year 657, in a description of the estates given by King Wulfhere to the Abbey of Peterborough. (1) Today the mere no longer exists, except in name, yet its influence is still strong – in the landscape and in local tradition and in folk memory.

In the following pages we have tried to bring back to life some of the Mere's past interest and importance and open a door into this fascinating present day world.

Origins &
Natural History

"Rather an awkward place to go to see: for being surrounded by a tract of perfectly fenny country and screened moreover by a phalanx of tall reeds near the margins of the water, the nearer you approach the lake itself, the less able you are to get a view of it." (2)

Whittlesea Mere was once the largest freshwater lake in lowland Britain, covering upwards of 2,000 (c 850 hectares) acres of low-lying peat fen in the old county of Huntingdonshire. Recent research has demonstrated the beginnings of mere formation in the Holme Fen area during the Mesolithic period, although the origins of Whittlesea Mere itself seem to date from the late Iron Age/Roman period. Certainly by the end of the Iron Age, the Holme Fen area was a raised bog whose vegetation was more reminiscent of the Yorkshire Moors than of the low-lying fens as we know them today.

This raised bog had built up over thousands of years to such an extent that the river Nene, flowing downstream past Farcet and Yaxley, had been channelled to turn at right angles across the fen, meandering towards Ramsey St. Mary's (see map). The streams running down from the hills behind Stilton seeped through the raised bog and merged with the Nene on its leisurely progress to the sea.

Some time towards the end of the Roman period a rise in sea level led to extensive flooding and thick silt deposits were laid down around Wisbech and Spalding, and well up the river valleys as far as Peterborough on the Nene and Welney on the old course of the Great Ouse. The result was that the Nene became embanked by silt levees, which dammed back the upland streams. The shifting pattern of open water, fen and bog slowly formed a landscape with permanent meres of which Whittlesea was the largest,

How Big was Whittlesea Mere?

"Here for six miles in length and three in breadth
that cleer, deepe and fishfull Mere named
Witlesmere spreadeth itself"

William Camden, writing at the beginning of the seventeenth century, so reckoned the extent of Whittlesea Mere. Although these dimensions have been repeated over time, for instance by Celia Fiennes, the great traveller on horseback, who came upon the Mere riding from Huntingdon to Stilton in 1697, it has been generally agreed that such dimensions are impossible to credit. The superb silk map of the Mere, published by John Bodger in 1786 (see centre spread), estimated the mere bed at 1570 square acres and approximately two miles by one and a half miles in extent, whilst two nineteenth century sources came up with dimensions of five miles by two miles, and two and a half miles by one and three quarter miles.

How can we reconcile these varying figures?

It is inevitable that, as fenland drainage progressed from later medieval schemes, such as Moreton's Leam, to the general draining of the seventeenth century and the introduction of more and more effective wind and then steam powered drainage mills, there will have been a generalised drying out of the fenland peats. This must have had a significant impact on areas of open water, such as Whittlesea Mere.

Indeed, William Dugdale, writing in the mid-seventeenth century, published two maps of Whittlesea Mere, one of the pre-drainage "drowned Fenn" with the circumference of the Mere approximately eleven and three quarter miles, and the other post-drainage, when he recorded the circumference of the Mere as approximately seven and a half miles. So we can readily believe that by the late 18th century, Whittlesea Mere may have been much smaller than in medieval times.

Another factor which will have come into play was seasonal variation in the water levels. An enquiry of 1564, concerned with establishing property boundaries in the parish of Farcet, noted several witness statements that, for the past forty years, *"Wytlesmere doth at certain tymes in the yeare yearlie and especiallie in winter time surround, weare, waste and wynne of the said pasture called Farcett Fenn."*

Nevertheless, it is still hard to believe that the area of open water was ever, even at times of high flood, so large as Camden and Fiennes recorded. As the Victoria County History indicates (see Further Reading), such extensive dimensions would take the mere from Horsey Hill in the north all the way to south of Hooks Lode, beyond Holme village, in the south!

Whilst accepting seasonal variation and steady decline in the body of

The Great Fen Project

In the 2000s a major 50-100 year re-wilding project was established, working to restore a wetland landscape to 3700 hectares of fenland around the two existing national nature reserves of Holme Fen and Woodwalton Fen. Working with landowners and farmers, this project is re-creating a range of habitats which are seeing the re-establishment of plant and insect communities not seen since the drainage of the meres in the mid-19th century. Although Whittlesea Mere itself cannot be brought back, something of the rich diversity of wildlife supported by the undrained fen, is returning for all to enjoy.

www.greatfen.org.uk

water as the draining of the fens progressed, perhaps the key factor was something concerned with changing perceptions of what constituted "Whittlesea Mere".

In medieval times, as is clear in the records of the fenland abbeys like Peterborough, Ramsey and Thorney, major landscape features were frequently taken as shorthand for larger blocks of fen lands. The 12th century Peterborough monk, Hugh Candidus, set out the bounds of Peterborough's holdings in the fens *"with the meres and lakes of Scelfremere and Whittlesea Mere and all others however many thereunto belonging.."*

It is more than likely therefore that Camden had picked up on records to the area around Whittlesea Mere, characterised by its rich pasture, turf pits and fisheries, whose dimensions concerned a region, not solely the open water. Viewed in these terms as an area, whose main feature was the mere, then "Whittlesea Mere", measuring six miles by three miles is not impossible – bounded by hills and upland to the west, and by Kingsdelph to the east, in essence the bay of fen sited south of the modern villages of Farcet and Yaxley.

So, how big was Whittlesea Mere? Bigger than we might think!!

Natural History

Imagine a vast expanse of water stretching some three miles by two miles (approximately five by three kilometres), no more than seven feet (2.1 metres) deep, surrounded by a thick belt of reed and sedge swamp and fed by small channels of water. On the Mere itself, an abundance of wildfowl and at dusk black clouds of starlings flying in to roost in the reed shoals, whilst on the fringes of the Mere one or two mereside cottages where fishing nets are laid out to dry.

Venturing up one of the narrow lodes, the brilliant flash of dragonflies and the more leisured and random flight of butterflies catches the eye against the bankside vegetation's collage of colour. Our approach suddenly flushes a wisp of snipe into the air from the hassocks of grass in the heathered bog which stretches away towards Holme village. It seems a desolate and eerily beautiful scene, remote from civilisation.

Imagine too, the reed and sedge cutters coming out from Yaxley and Holme to spend back-breaking, chilling hours harvesting the crops of reed on to rafts and then leading the rafts up the lode to the stacking yards; the turf cutter digging blocks of peat for winter fires; the shout of a horse boy, his imagination excited by the open expanse of the Mere, turns our gaze towards a gang of lighters carrying coal across the Mere on its way from the yards at Yaxley to Ramsey town.

This was nature's landscape but one that admitted men and women into an intimate partnership with it. Without the Mere and the bog, without the crops of reed and grass and peat, the way of life of the villagers would have been less rich and varied. Without the people to manage the reed beds and to clear the river channels and control the grazing of pasture, the Mere and fen would have silted and dried up long before drainage finally took place in 1851.

Contemporary descriptions of the Holme Fen area illustrate how rich the fen was in plants, many of which are now extinct in the area. John

Bog Oaks

Bog oaks, as seen by John Bliss and others who have worked the land in the fens, used to be a common sight after ploughing in the peat fens, as the plough struck and pulled up the buried trunks of trees from the peat which had overwhelmed them centuries ago. Over the years, the accumulation of decaying vegetation, itself the essential ingredient of peat formation, raised the surface of the land above the water table of seasonally flooded fens, enabling shrubs and then trees to colonise and become established. The forests which grew were composed initially of damp tolerant trees such as willow and alder, but gradually birch, oak and ash also grew. Renewed periods of flooding starved the trees of nutrients and the trees died, becoming in time buried as renewed peat formation began within the flooded area, and so the cycle began all over again. In some parts of the fens, several "horizons" of tree growth are found through the great depths of peat, showing how this landscape has never been static, rather a dynamic mosaic of shifting meres, reed shoals and grasslands with shrubs and trees.

Clare, the Helpston poet, with a sensitive eye for detail, wrote in a letter in March 1825:

"In fact we have many ferns. There is a beautiful one which a friend of mine calls the 'Lady Fern' growing among the boggy spots on Whittlesea Mere and a dwarf willow grows there about a foot high which it never exceeds. It is also a place very common for the cranberry that trails by the brink of the mere. There are several water weeds too with very beautiful or peculiar flowers that have not yet been honoured with christnings from modern botany." (3)

Although drainage of the Mere and subsequent farming has changed the landscape markedly from these early descriptions, in some places the plants typical of the bog do manage to survive. Holme Fen, a 658 acre (275 hectare) nature reserve, is dominated by birch forest, but present day management is creating conditions in which 'lost' species can re-establish themselves. Nearby, Woodwalton Fen, established in the early 20th century as a nature reserve, is also a rich remnant of the pre-drainage landscape. The ability of plant seeds to lie dormant for many years is well known, but it is still remarkable and a delight to see a woodland clearing produce a colourful flush of heather within two years of opening up the area. Elsewhere sphagnum moss, saw sedge and stinking gale (bog myrtle), all typical of the pre-drainage era, still occur.

Even on the Mere bed itself, and in Yaxley Fen, where cultivation has been continuous since drainage, the cutting and cleaning of dykes, or the removal of bog oaks from the fields, brings to the surface buried seed invariably described as oily, and green as the day it was buried. John Bliss, who farmed part of the Mere bed, describes his own experience:

"The most interesting thing is digging bog oaks out. You get all sorts of weed seeds out from six foot down ... all sorts of things that you don't see nowadays. Some quite strange."

(Interview 27 May 1986)

Farmers in Yaxley Fen report flag iris, bog rush and other unusual plants growing in the side of freshly cut dykes, where buried seed is germinated by exposure to the air. An unusual story was recorded by the Reverend Nowers, chaplain to the railway navvies who built the line across Holme Fen, of an acorn recovered from a few feet down in the peat, which grew into a seedling oak before dying. All these examples are reminders of the landscape of one hundred and fifty years ago and the potential for regeneration.

Whittlesea Mere and its vicinity was also renowned for certain rare species of moth and butterfly, which drew collectors from as far afield as London. These visitors provided a welcome additional income for local people whom they employed as guides, often giving them nicknames in their diaries and jottings, as when the Reverend Bree dubbed his guide 'Copperface' during his rambles in 1840. Reed cutters in Yaxley collected and sold the larvae of the Reed Tussock or Whittlesea Satin Moth at a shilling per dozen and gypsies regularly netted specimen butterflies to sell to visiting collectors. The best known and most prized of the local species was the Large Copper Butterfly, now extinct, although the similar Dutch sub-species was introduced for a short time at nearby Woodwalton Fen. In 1851, a Mr. Shelton of Yaxley described himself as a collector of insects and was probably also a supplier to collectors from further afield. (4)

The drainage of the Meres destroyed much of the habitat on which these insects depended and the Whittlesea Satin Moth and Large Copper Butterfly have been lost. Nevertheless, the interest and rarity of a few species has continued to attract attention, as in the Huntingdonshire moth-hunting case of 1906 when four young men were sued for damages caused whilst hunting rare moths in Holme Wood. (5) The defendants, one June night, had erected a sheet and a lamp across a drove, thereby, it was claimed, disturbing the peaceful roost of 600 pheasants. The judge was evidently unimpressed and dismissed the case as a 'contemptible proceeding', having as little regard for the pheasants' sleep as for the survival of the rare moths!

Today, Holme Fen and nearby Woodwalton Fen still have some remarkable survivals of the pre-drainage landscape flora and fauna. The rare fen woodrush, only ever recorded in the Huntingdonshire fens, is still present at both reserves; the creeping willow, described by John Clare, along with sphagnum moss, heather and bog myrtle, all plants typical of the raised bog conditions which existed, are still to be found at Holme Fen. (See Appendix A)

A species count of butterflies, moths and dragonflies shows that both reserves are relatively rich – almost every category includes some rare or restricted example. Of course, a number of moths, like the better known butterflies, succumbed to the combined onslaught of reduced habitat and specimen collectors. But, in fact, very few of the key food plants have become extinct (see Appendix B) and the impression is left that dragonflies fared better in a declining natural habitat because they were less attractive to collectors than moths or butterflies. The irridescent blue of the magnificent Emperor dragonfly is a more common sight at Holme, having colonised the new mere in the reserve and the beautiful red Ruddy Darter, only a few years ago a nationally rare species, was by the late 1980s well established at both Holme and Woodwalton and had come off the rarity list.

A similar story of bare survival followed by recent growth of populations can be charted for nesting birds. At both reserves, the number of breeding bird species exceeds seventy and the birds typical of the vicinity of Whittlesea Mere are more and more in evidence – the snipe nests at Woodwalton Fen and is a visitor to Holme reserve; mallard, teal, gadwall and tufted duck nest at Holme Fen and are joined by visiting wigeon, shoveler and goldeneye. The new meres at Holme, dug as part of the reserve's management plan, with their associated reed beds, increased the reed and sedge warbler populations markedly and have certainly been instrumental in re-establishing a stable heronry since the mid-1970's. Even the bittern, regularly shot for sport in the days before the Mere was drained, is again a visitor at Woodwalton, where it is now successfully breeding, and occasionally recorded at Holme.

Over recent years the natural history interest of the Holme Fen area has continued to increase and once again it is attracting specialist naturalists. But though the booming bittern will perhaps be heard with more frequency as the new meres and their reed beds become established, Whittlesea Mere and its raised bog will never return. Today's examples are only an echo of the area's former glory.

Mere Living

To some upland visitors, Whittlesea Mere was a large unproductive wasteland all too prone to breed malarial mosquitos, the carriers of the infamous fen ague. But to the communities nearby , the waters of the Mere provided fish, wildfowl, reed and sedge; nourished the lush summer pastures, which fed huge stocks of cattle from communities on the fen edge and beyond and created a self-replenishing source of fuel in the peat beds. Pigot's Directory of 1840, under the entry for Yaxley, noted the Mere with its abundant fishery, and went on, *'the neighbourhood produces a great quantity of sedges and reeds in the preparation of which many persons find employment.'* Looking at 19th century census details it is surprising then how few individuals professed occupations directly connected with the Mere, as the following table shows:

	Yaxley	Holme
Turf dealer	1	–
Turf merchant	2	–
Carrier of turf	–	1
Reed/Sedge cutter	2	4
Reed merchant	1	1
Decoyman	–	1
Boatman	1	1

(Sources : 1841 census returns)

14

But these figures fail to reveal the important area of common right by which many local people had a share in the use of nature's gifts. The significance of these rights can be gauged by the tenacity with which they were defended when Holme Fen was the scene of a direct clash of interest between the local community and the new thrust for drainage improvement in the 17th century.

> *"At the time of the drivinge of the ffenns, Mr. Castle of Glatton, a Justice of the Peace, came into the ffen and told him (the drainers' overseer) that none of his (Mr. Castle's) cattell should be driven thence; yet the overseer going on with his drift, Mr. Castle appointed two of his men to stand in the gapp where the cattell should passe and kept them from going out; and he stood by while a great many women and men with sithes and pitchforkes gave many threateninge wordes that they would iette out the gutts of anie one that should drive theyr ffenns." (6)*

Nor was all sweet harmony between neighbouring communities, as local court rolls reveal, with their catalogue of offences of trespass and theft – in 1308, Thomas, son of Agnes of Holme, accused the men of Denton of carrying off his turves *"to his injury"*. (7) It was the potentially violent competition for valuable land that perhaps led Turkill the Dane during the reign of Cnut to divide the fen between the villages, marking their respective grounds with 'clear boundaries and divisions'. (8) We can still see the effects of this division in the narrow wedge-shaped parishes of Stilton, Caldecote and Denton, each of them guaranteed access to fen pasture and with a share of the Mere shore.

On the eastern side of the Mere a similar boundary was necessary to keep the monks of Ramsey and Thomey Abbeys apart. The quarrel arose over respective rights for pasturing of stock, and Small Dyke, which was dug as a result (itself almost certainly an ironic name, since the dyke was substantially wider than the normal width), still leaves its mark on the landscape as the parish boundary between Farcet and Ramsey. By the agreement of April/ May 1224 each monastery undertook to maintain its own side of the sixteen foot wide dyke. (9)

Fishing

Medieval Fenland was famous for its fisheries and, in particular, its eels (Ely probably means eel island). At the time of Domesday, Doddington returned 27,150 eels as an annual rental to Ely Abbey and this was a fraction of the total available to the monks. Eels were reckoned by 'the stick' pierced through the gills of twenty five eels, and must have been an all too regular dish on the monks' dinner table. But the value of the fishery was not only in varying the home menu, it was also a useful source of revenue when leased out to others. A late 17th century sale of one fishery on the Mere was priced at £55, the modern equivalent being well in excess of £10,000. Even as late as 1812 the Dean and Chapter of Peterborough Cathedral renewed a long-running lease for a two acre close associated with two 'boatgates' which entitled the lessee to carefully defined fishing rights at the southern edge of Whittlesea Mere. In return they asked for an annual rent of forty shillings and "*one dish of fresh ffish or ffour shillings in money payable at or in the Great West Porch of the Cathedral Church.*" (10) The best of both worlds!

> *"In Witelsmare the Abbot of Ramsey has one boat, and the Abbot of Peterborough one boat and the Abbot of Thorney two boats. One of these two boats and two fisheries and two fishermen and one virgate (about 20 acres) of land, the Abbot of Peterborough*

holds from the Abbot of Thorney ... The fisheries and meres
of the Abbot of Ramsey in Huntingdonshire are valued at £10,
those of the Abbot of Thomey at 60 shillings, those of the Abbot of
Peterborough at £4."

Domesday Book, Hunts. 205a

The commercial fishing rights on the Mere were defined in terms of 'boats' or 'boatgates' of which there were fifteen at the time of drainage. A document in 1306 noted by John Bodger on his map of Whittlesea Mere, gave right of fishing at all times except during Shelerode, which lasted for a fortnight either side of St. George's Day. The lessee was entitled to use a variety of nets and trawls which leave one wondering how any fish survived! Each boatgate authorised the use of 40 polenets, 40 swerenets, 24 widenets, 24 bownets, 1 drage, 1 tramaile and the right of setting tawe and syrelepes at will. Even though we cannot be sure of the exact nature of each of these devices, their effect on the fish must have been considerable, serving to underline the richness of the Mere's fishery.

The fishermen themselves, first mentioned in Domesday, appear to have been fully employed by the Mere. We find mention of the King, in 1318, granting permission for the construction of a cottage in the marsh of Glatton beside the waters of Wytlesmere where the fishermen could spread their nets out to dry and save themselves *"in time of tempest which often happens here."* (11)

Archaeology has revealed the traces of their cottages with large collections of medieval kitchen wares showing that meals were prepared and eaten by the Mere, and some of the tools of the trade – lead weights and sharpening stones. These fishermen were, by the nature of their trade, solitary men, independent and self reliant, as this 17th century poetic description reveals:

"Here (Frog Hall) in ancestral halls has Norman long
Dwelt huge, ungainly, maim'd but angler strong;
He spreads his nets alike for pike and eels,
Makes laws at pleasure and again repeals." (12)

The fishing was, in fact, carefully controlled and this was the responsibility of the 'Fennifers' (originally a term applied to the fishermen themselves) who were appointed each year by the manor court of Glatton cum Holme (Holme only became a separate parish in 1857). They were empowered to enact local byelaws and levy fines through the court to back up those orders. In 1662 four men described as 'piscatores de le Mere' were fined four shillings simply for failing to attend the court, and in the same year night fishing was outlawed by an order instructing fishermen on the Mere not to raise their nets before sunrise, on threat of the enormous fine for each offence of forty shillings. (13) The last of the independent fishermen directly associated with the Mere was Oakey Phillips, who never did anything but fish the Mere. He was in his fifties when the Mere was drained, and sadly was unable to adapt to a new life. He emigrated to America and died there.

During the last years of the Mere's existence, the fishing was divided between four men – Joseph Coles had the Yaxley side, Ralph Bradford the Farcet side, Bellamy Bradford the Bevill's Leam side and John Coles the Holme side. Bownets were used to catch pike in March, bream in May and tench in July, after which time baited lines were used to catch eels by the hundred. When the Mere was drained the water gradually receded over a three week period leaving the fish concentrated in the deepest waters around Swere Point, midway on the southern side. John Coles' last harvest of fish was described in a newspaper report:

"He had a net made about 100 yards long, 4 feet deep, bunged at
the top and leaded at the bottom, and where the water was about

two and a half feet deep , he fastened one end of the net to one end of a large boat which nearly touched the bottom, and where he thought the fish were collected he would run the net out with a small fishing boat straight and then bring it round in a circle to the other end of the boat, so encircling the fish ... When they had reduced the circle to about eight yards across, it was a sight to see the fish . They were so thickly crammed together that in struggling they actually knocked each other over the top of the net – pike as much as 18lb each, bream 3lb and 4lb each, tench 4lb each and 5lb each, roach , rudd and perch big too. Mr. Coles said there were two tons of fish in the net. He had a spring wagon and two carts which they filled with fish in hampers till they would hold no more. About a ton weight was sent off at one." (14)

Fowling & Reed Cutting

John and Joseph Coles between them paid £700 a year to William Wells, Lord of the Manor, for the rights of fishing, wildfowling and reed cutting on the Mere. They, like many, found these three jobs complementary seasonal activities. (15)

Fowlers on the Mere used a flintlock gun fastened to, and extending beyond the prow of the low punt-like boat. The fowler put his hands over the side of the boat, laying on his front, and holding an eighteen inch paddle in each hand. In this way he could propel the boat silently through the water and could approach the wildfowl unheard. Only one shot was possible with such a gun, since its report would scare all the wildflow away but although crude in its operation, these fowlers, so Joseph Coles recorded, successfully shot large numbers of birds. William Sharman once picked up twenty seven dead birds after a single shot.

Wildfowling with a punt gun on a stalking sledge on Whittlesea Mere (J.M. Heathcote).
Note: Peterborough Cathedral in background. The punt gun and long quant (punt pole).

A more subtle and certain method of catching wildfowl was introduced to the area in 1815 when John Shelton started to work the Holme Fen decoy just south of the Mere. By luring the birds from the central open pond along a net covered 'pipe', the fowl could be panicked into headlong flight into the netting at the narrowed end of the pipe. In this way huge numbers of birds (2,400 duck in one week) were caught and despatched to Leadenhall Market in London where they sold at eight shillings a couple.

Other birds than wildfowl were to be found at local dinner tables . Starlings, sold by the sackful at 6d a dozen, were a common sight and were a regular addition to the diet as remembered in this childhood rhyme from Yaxley:

Duck Decoys

The introduction of engineered ponds, designed specifically for luring and catching wildfowl, dates in England from the 17th century and seems to be a by-product of Dutch involvement in the fenland drainage schemes of that time. An area of open water was linked to a series of curved channels (usually between 4 and 6), each of which was covered with netting and became progressively narrower towards the end. Depending on the wind direction, a particular channel or "pipe" would be used and wing-clipped birds, kept on the water for the purpose, would be trained to respond to feed being scattered at the entrance to the selected pipe by swimming along the channel. This would, in turn, entice any wild birds which had arrived on the water, into the pipe. Along the pipe, the decoyman had erected reed panels, behind which he could hide from the open water, so as not to scare the birds. Between each screen however, a low screen was placed, over which the decoyman's dog, traditionally called Piper, would be trained to jump, running away from the water and towards the narrow end of the pipe. As the dog leapt each jump, it would appear and disappear from view to the wildfowl, whose natural curiosity drew them towards the retreating creature. The trained birds would have seen all this before and would carry on feeding, but wild birds evidently could not resist investigating further. In the event that the wild birds took wind, on turning to retreat out of the pipe, they would be confronted by a full view of the decoyman and eventually would be panicked into flight down the pipe and into the prepared keepnet at the end, from which they could be extracted, killed and sent off to market. A fully working decoy still exists in the fens, near Peterborough at Newborough [Cook and Pilcher 1982]

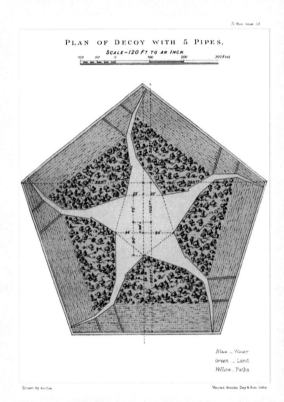

PLAN OF DECOY WITH 5 PIPES.
SCALE-120 FT TO AN INCH.

Blue _ Water
Green _ Land
Yellow _ Paths

"Starling pie hot
Starling pie cold
Starling pie all the week
Till ten days old"

The starlings were the great enemy of the reed cutters, breaking down the reeds as they roosted in their thousands among the reed beds around Whittlesea Mere. Local reed merchants employed boys to scare the birds during the day in order to minimise the damage but this could be a dangerous job as the story of John Beharral shows.

Ten year old John, a pupil at Holme National School, was bird scaring one Sunday in February 1851. Whilst walking amongst the reeds he was collecting 'cats tail', the feathery seed of the reed-mace which was used locally to stuff pillows. Suddenly he realised that he was sinking into the soft mud and, unable to extricate himself, he sank inch by inch until he came to a stop with the mud up to his armpits.

It was then half past three in the afternoon. He shouted for help but no one was about and all he could do was mark the passage of time by the striking of Conington church clock and the sounds of the trains on the nearby Great Northern Railway.

By the Monday morning John was too cold and numb to raise a shout, even though he occasionally glimpsed movements of labourers. At ten o'clock he heard someone moving about just beyond the reeds but was powerless to attract his attention and could only listen in growing despair as the sounds of movement receded in the distance. Then, half an hour later, the same man returned and came straight to the spot where John's head, shoulders and arms could be seen above the mud. With difficulty the man released John from his nineteen hour ordeal and carried him home to his parents who all the while had assumed that John had walked to see his grandmother in Sawtry! A doctor was called and after a week all outward signs of the experience had gone and John returned to school none the worse for his adventure. Asked later why he had returned to the particular spot in the reed bed, the

Holme Lode in winter. Note the reed and peat stacks (J.M. Heathcote)

man who found John said he did not know, only that he felt he had to go back as if guided by some unseen power.

The reed harvest that John Beharral was helping to protect was the other great crop provided by the Mere in addition to fish and fowl. In 1841 Holme village had four cutters and one reed merchant, whilst Yaxley had two known cutters and Joseph Coles, the reed merchant. The Farcet farmer, Bellamy Bradford, also dealt in reeds from the Mere.

Harvest began when the first frosts of winter had killed the leaf, and bundles of reed rapidly built up at the head of Holme lode and in the yards at Yaxley. The stacks at Holme in 1851 were valued at no less than £1,300, the staggering modern equivalent of almost £150,000! Apart from its use in thatching local houses, the reed was carted over long distances into Northamptonshire, and north to Derbyshire and Nottinghamshire. Sometimes the carts arrived loaded with pottery or besoms which were sold in the Peterborough area before loading up with reed for the return journey. Joseph Coles used to tell the story of how he accompanied the wagons carrying the reed from Whittlesea

Mere all the way down to London and on to Dover, from which port it was shipped to France.

Reed was also used in temporary fencing, brick making, plastered ceilings and internal house walls (some of these still survive in older farms in the area) and even as an underlay for parlour floors. In winter, reeds were commonly used to dry up the muddy yards around the farms. As might be expected, the reed beds declined in value once the Mere was drained and the land began to dry out. In 1867 the last commercial crop was taken and it must have been an incredulous audience of children that listened to John Beharral as he recounted his muddy ordeal in the reed shoal.

Mere Leisure

"We recommend frozen out lovers of hunting, coursing and horse racing, during this frost, to take a trip to Peterborough and they will find good sport on the ice, particularly on Whittlesea Mere." (16)

The Mere was famed for its recreational fishing and shooting and was a regular attraction for leisured gentlemen of the area and working people alike. Heathcote's weekend parties at Conington Castle always included a day's sport on the Mere for which variety was the keynote. Depending on the season, it was possible to skate, go ice-boating, sailing, fishing, shooting, insect and plant specimen collecting or sketching. Students from Cambridge made the Mere a regular fixture in their social calendar.

"My friend Hopkins and I always spent a week in August with Berry who rented the Mere. We paid him 7 shillings each pr day for Board and Lodging and spent our time in Shooting Flappers, Moorhens and Halfers."

Thomas Rooper, 12 November 1864 (17)

Adam Sedgwick, the great geologist, also made his first acquaintance with the Mere as a student at Cambridge. In 1809 by way of a bravado he set out after a supper party at St. John's College and walked for over seven hours through the night to join a fishing party at the Mere.

What he managed to catch we do not know, but pike of 20 to 30 lbs were often landed though few approached the record breaking 52 pounder (it was four feet seven inches long) caught during the last years of the Mere's existence. (18)

The highlight of the summer season fell on the second Tuesday in June when The Feast of the New Club regatta was held. Hundreds of local worthies sailed on the Mere in a great fleet of boats and competed for various prizes. Picnics, brass bands and dancing at Swere Point and Black Ham were a feature of the day with prime viewing stations for the races being settled on early in the day. Occasionally the finery of the situation was spoiled by the weather:

"The morning was remarkably fine and the placid mere was glided over by upwards of 80 pleasure boats of various sizes and descriptions containing 1,000 persons, many of whom were fashionable well dressed ladies ... the scene was changed to one of disappointment and perplexity about one o'clock by a thunderstorm , attended by a heavy downfall of rain which

The Feast of the New Club regatta, held on Whittlesea Mere

lasted four hours in succession. The ladies' dresses were literally drenched , the boats were nearly half filled with water and the only alternative was to recross the Mere." (19)

The influx of visitors to the area at such social high points of the year meant a source of income for local people which could be a welcome addition to the everyday rewards of work in that area. Visitors staying in the area would lodge with a local farmer or at the Chequers Inn, Yaxley. Doris Rootham of Ramsey St. Mary recalls how her grandfather, a turf cutter at Holme, used to take people for boat trips.

"He had his own boat. Before all the fen were drained, all round Ladyseat and those farms just below Slote's, he used to take people for picnics round on his boat. The people he took nearly every Sunday. Grandmother – he'd draw up at the side of the bank and then she'd make a cup of tea . And they brought grandmother that green tea service cos she'd been so kind to them. The people come from all over – Thorney and different parts. They come on a pony and trap."

Interview 23 February 1986

Mr. Carter, the turf cutter in question, was born in the 1820's and was always in the "picnic business". Ladyseat Farm lies on the southern edge of what was Whittlesea Mere. So we have here a story, passed down through the family, of Sunday afternoon picnics on the Mere enjoyed by the better-off families from nearby villages. This tradition of recreational use certainly outlived the Mere itself, for, in another conversation, Doris and her sister Olive Taylor, confirmed that they had been told of boat trips having taken place in the 1850's, and perhaps later, on the last remaining waters of Ugg Mere. In fact, Ugg Mere was drained during the 1830s, but this family tradition may nevertheless record the ongoing pleasure boating, now confined to the river channels, with passengers no doubt entertained with stories of the mere before drainage. Such information gives a rare insight into the regular enjoyment of these fenland meres, and balances the better documented but much less frequent water extravaganzas such as the one held in August 1669 by the then Lord of the Manor of Orton Longueville, William Pierrepont. His guests were the Dean and Chapter of the cathedral and after a leisurely cruise, the clergy-filled vessel dropped anchor off Frog Hall on the northern side of the Mere and set to on a magnificent feast starting with melon, followed by venison, beef, mutton and savoury pasties, chicken and pork, then followed by salt hams, tongues and bacon. The sweets included fresh fruit, cheesecakes and wafers. Cider or wine were liberally provided to wash the feast down. (20)

For many local people, the diversions afforded by the Mere were the nearest thing to a holiday that any of them could hope for – as Joseph Coles of Yaxley mused, thinking of his young days when the Mere was still there – *"there were no cheap railway excursions to the seaside in those days."*

Now and again an unusual visitor was recorded, as when a Norwich clergyman sailed his cutter 'The Bure' on to the Mere, only to be stranded by a fall in the water level towards the end of summer. The unfortunate vicar seems not to have enjoyed his enforced stay, for when re-visited in October he lamented *"Oh Sir, this is perfect banishment. I have seen nothing but peat barges since you left."* In despair of ever escaping, he sold his boat for £120 to Lord Hinchingbrooke and Mr. Heathcote who used it for summer fishing parties. (21)

Some thirty years earlier in July and August 1774, Lord Orford chronicled his journey along the fen rivers and across the Mere. (22) Lord Orford was the grandson of Sir Robert Walpole and inherited Houghton Hall in Norfolk, but his interests lay neither in politics nor estate management. A keen gambler, his eccentricities led him into 'toad-like' passions – now ballooning, now sailing – and he is said to have considered a week utterly lost if he had not spent two or three nights aboard ship.

It was in the wake of Lord Anson's return from a world voyage and hard on news that Thomas Cook was wintering in New Zealand on his second round-the-world voyage that George, Lord Orford, set out to chart the fenland waterways. With the passion of schoolboys, he and his crew regarded the countryside through which they passed as uncharted territory, giving blunt descriptions of the 'natives' whom they encountered, naming significant landmarks after each other, and earnestly fearing the worst after the failure of one of their number to return at the appointed hour *"on account of the late reports from New Zealand"*. He had, in fact , gone to visit a friend at Ramsey!

The pretence was dropped once they arrived in the Mere for here was the serious business of visiting the races at Peterborough, attending the theatre and entertaining local dignitaries, and enjoying the sport of the Mere itself. On 25 July, Lord Orford welcomed on board the Earl of Sandwich and together they dined on the day's catch – twenty brace of pike and perch.

George clearly enjoyed his visit, for the following year he wrote to the Earl proposing a wager on a one or two-man boat race across the Mere.

"My Dr Lord. 4 July 1775

I trouble you with this note to acquaint you that I propose cruising on Whittlesea Mere with the Squadron under my command between Peterborough and Huntingdon races ... If you approve of it I will join with your Lordship in a prize of five or ten Guineas to be given any day you shall fix towards the back of this month ... please order bills to be presented at Huntingdon and dispersed about the villages bordering on the Mere." (23)

In winter time, too, there was considerable activity on the Mere as the reed sledges were brought out for pleasure, and people put on their skates.

In the winter of 1822/3 an ice fair was held on the Mere itself with carts, donkeys, booths and chestnut sellers forming a focus of activity alongside the skating races. John Bodger, on his famous map of the Mere, also mentions ice-boat sailing on the frozen Mere, which was justly regarded as a theatre of ice sports. According to Heathcote and others who knew the Mere, scarcely a day went past, conditions permitting, without an event of some kind being organised with a prize of a new hat, a pig, a leg of mutton or a purse of £5 or £10 being offered.

"There was an exciting contest on Tuesday last between two crack skaters, one named Register (alias Flying Dutchman), and the other named Barnes; the stakes being £10 a side. At the signal for starting, both competitors went off at a good pace against a strong head wind; and during the whole distance the issue was doubtful. The distance (two miles) was run in 7 min. 7 secs (and was won by Register) ... we noticed among the visitors ... the Earl of FitzWilliam and the Ladies FitzWilliam who have liberally contributed towards these sports." (24)

When the Mere was drained; many looked back with regret for the enjoyment that had been lost:

Illustrated London News

"Whittlesea Mere was a scene of interest to the visitor both to the painter, sportsman and the naturalist. One now looks in vain for that broad expanse of water reflecting the grey passing clouds and margined with vast masses of reed and sedge ... how fine were those bright, broad-leaved and cup-like flowers through which we poled our little punt. The towers of the cathedral, the neighbouring spires and the numerous and highly picturesque water mills and their clicking machinery – all these were charms for which we now seek in vain , but which we can never forget." (25)

E. W. Cooke, 27 September 1875

Whilst much has changed, as we saw earlier, something of the plant life does survive and the wildfowl are returning. Although the Mere no longer freezes over, the tradition of skating has continued in many families and races still take place, when the ice permits, on the washes at Dog in a Doublet. Fishing, too, is a major attraction of the area as anyone who has driven along North Bank, Whittlesey at the weekend, will know.

Cutting the engine drain across the bed of Whittlesea Mere.
Note Yaxley church on the horizon (Illustrated London News)

31

Draining the Mere

Whittlesea Mere, even at its lowest ebb, was more than four times the size of Hickling Broad, but by the middle of the 19th century its great days were over. Progressive drainage since the 17th century in the Cambridgeshire fens had steadily lowered the water level in the meres between Peterborough and Ramsey and already in the early 1800's thoughts of drainage were in the air, spurred on by the knowledge of good wheat crops and large profits to be gained from newly reclaimed fen soils.

Visitors to the Mere noted large areas of near stagnant water and in the hot summer of 1826 Whittlesea Mere dried up entirely, destroying the fishing for five years. Just ten years later, the engineer, John Rennie, found parts of the Mere bed overgrown with reed and scarcely a depth of six inches of water. In the face of this progressive silting and drying out, the rivers had been canalised on the south side of the Mere from Old Decoy Farm to Johnson's Point and the Yaxley lode was channelled round the edge of the diminishing Trundle Mere. It was even possible to lease part of the former bed near Swere Point as pasture. (26)

Various schemes were proposed for the total drainage and 'improvement' of the Mere and surrounding fen, and in 1845 the local landowners expressed their confidence in the outcome by entering into an agreement which divided the Mere bed between them. (27)

Finally the work began with the construction of a northern catchwater, now known as Black Ham River. This diverted all the

Appold's pump at Johnson's Point, veiwed from the Old Nene
(Illustrated London News).

waters of the Nene from the Mere and carried them into the 17th century watercourse of Bevill's Leam. By 1851 all was ready to begin emptying the Mere itself. Most of the water was run off by gravity at Foleaster Point on the north west side of the Mere into the newly dug Black Ham river. By March the Mere bed was sufficiently dry to commence work on cutting boundary dykes and digging the mill drain for a new pump which could guarantee the drainage of the newly reclaimed area. At the Great Exhibition of 1851, an inventor named Appold exhibited for the first time a working model of a centrifugal pump. It attracted much attention,

"pouring forth a voluminous cascade to the great delight of a constant throng of spectators."

Though the pump provided much amusement, there was a strong feeling expressed by many eminent engineers that it would prove to be nothing more than an ingenious toy.

However, William Wells, the Lord of the Manor of Glatton cum Holme, apparently saw the pump and was so impressed by its performance that he immediately arranged to have a pump twenty times larger than the exhibited model, constructed and installed for use in completing the drainage of the great Mere which had dominated his Huntingdonshire estates.

As October drew to a close all was ready and on 12 November 1851 a large party, including local landowners, engineers and designers, assembled at Johnson's Point to witness the opening of the pump house. A tent had been erected nearby, surmounted with flags and decorated with flowers and evergreens. An embroidered banner proclaimed:

"See proudly floats our flag on high
O'er wastes by history renowned.
All hail! the Mere at length is dry
Success has perserverance crowned."

and William Wells entertained his guests to a splendid luncheon amidst the machinery, to celebrate the achievement. (28)

Crowds of local people watched the whole operation, no doubt with mixed feelings, as a great focus of social and economic life was drained away before their eyes. Not slow to take an opportunity, however, many came with baskets, sacks and even carts to collect the fish left floundering in the mud.

Tons of pike, perch and eels were lifted by men, wearing boards strapped to their feet so that they did not sink into the mud. So great was the amount of stranded fish that thousands were left rotting in the mud.

Fish were not the only treasures to be taken from the Mere after it was drained, however. Resting on the Mere bed near the deep water channel which crossed the Mere from north to south, a collection of four massive stone blocks with mason's marks, and a number of smaller pieces were found. The story is told that the stones were destined for Ramsey Abbey, having been quarried at Barnack near Stamford, but that the lighter carrying them foundered in the shallows on the southern side of the Mere. Not surprisingly, since the individual blocks weigh about a ton each, the stones remained unmoved for many years. John Bliss takes up the story:

> *"The stones were there when my father took the farm over about 1919. Being rather a tidy man he decided that he didn't want them there and he loaded them up one at a time with a block and tackle and put one at a time in a horse and cart and brought them and put them in front of the house (Engine Farm). They were there until we took the house down. Then everybody wanted one and I decided that they should stay together and I concreted them all on a plinth round the yard so that anyone could see them and they'd stay put where they belonged."*
>
> *Interview 27 May 1986*

Most famous of all the discoveries was a silver censer and incense boat, decorated with the ram's head of Ramsey Abbey. Joseph Coles, the finder, told the story of his amazing find:

> *"When I first picked up the censer I knew it was something curious. I thought perhaps it was an ancient lamp. I brought it home and washed it well. I then tested it to see of what metal it was and we found it was made of solid silver and was washed with gold. The Mere had only been drained a few days when I found it and it was lying practically half in and half out of the mud, a pitcher was lying near it. My father and I went with it to Lord Northampton ... it was arranged that he was to give £50 for it, but Lord Northampton wrote to Mr. Wells about it and he, as Lord of the manor, at once claimed it and gave me £25 for finding*

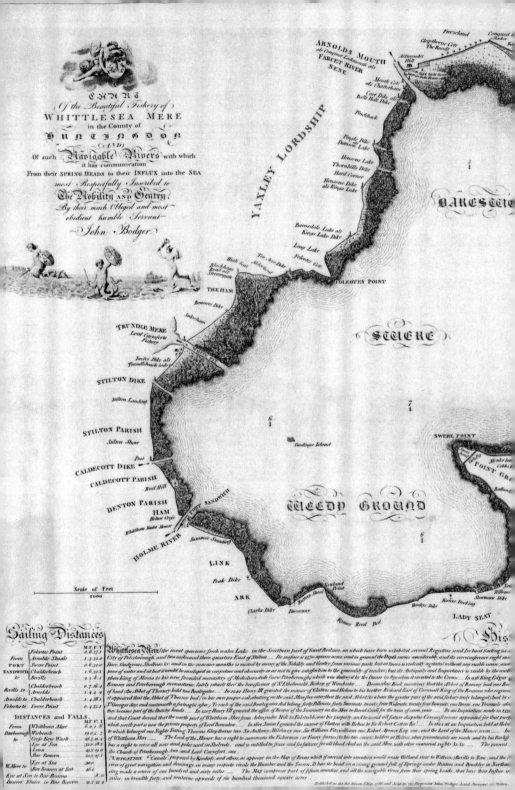

CHART Of the Beautiful Fishery of WHITTLESEA MERE in the County of HUNTINGDON AND Of such Navigable Rivers with which it has communication From their SPRING HEADS to their INFLUX into the SEA most Respectfully Inscribed to The Nobility and Gentry. By their much Obliged and most obedient humble Servant John Bodger.

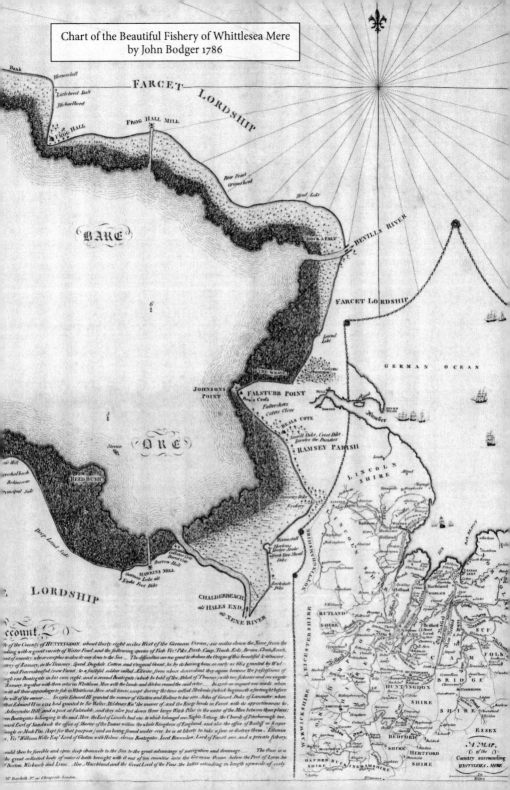

Chart of the Beautiful Fishery of Whittlesea Mere
by John Bodger 1786

it ... at the sale of Mr. Wells' things it was sold and was purchased by Lord Carysfort for £1,100 and it is at Elton Hall now." (29)

Such is life!

The year 1852 saw the start of the process of laying out of farm boundaries, new roads and field dykes. To aid consolidation of the Mere bed, crops of coleseed were sown but even so, large cracks appeared as the land slowly dried out. The north east and south west parts of the Mere were laid out first in neat rectangular blocks of fields. A triangular area, presumably the wettest (this was the area last fished by John Coles) was left around what is now Engine Farm and Tower Farm, and was the last to be divided up.

All seemed to be progressing well with the reclamation but on 12 November 1852 the drainers were shocked when heavy rains choked the new Appold pump and burst the banks of the new river. Suddenly Whittlesea Mere had returned and was three feet deep again. Local wild fowlers were quick to seize the opportunity, but it was a short-lived setback for the drainers. The pump successfully reclaimed the Mere to within a day of its predicted performance and this episode proved to be the last gasp of Whittlesea Mere. William Wells allowed himself a touch of exaggeration when he boasted:

"the wind which in the autumn of 1851 was curling the blue waters of the lake, in the autumn of 1853 was blowing in the same place over fields of yellow corn." (30)

The same mood of euphoria was caught by the editors of the Illustrated London News:

"After having been accustomed for so many years to see Whittlesea Mere as nothing but a flat scene – fenny, watery, swampy and unproductive – it will be almost startling to see, at the touch of the genius of improvement, the water flow into canals, the swamps

become green pasture grounds, the fens flooded over with a golden sea of ripened corn, and farms and homesteads gathering round them the treasures of the soil." (31)

The last of the Fenland Meres had been drained.

After the Mere

After the euphoria of the successful drainage with its promise of new agricultural land coming under cultivation, the hard business of getting the land ditched and parcelled and prepared for cropping began. It soon became clear that the acidic peats of Holme Fen presented a much greater challenge than the silt bed of the mere itself, and despite extensive preparation, by paring off the fibrous top layers of peat, burning and mixing the ash into the underlying softer peat, further regular claying or warping was essential to combat the acidity of the raised bog peat if grain crops were to be successfully taken from the newly reclaimed land. This involved transporting cart loads of the shell marl from the mere bed onto the peatlands from one direction, and clay quarried from around the village of Holme to other parts of the raised bog which lay nearer to the upland. Horse and cart were augmented by the installation of a narrow gauge rail track to speed the process.

A massive investment of financial capital was necessary and over the course of the next two decades, William Wells was not only able to celebrate the successful cultivation of a large acreage which had previously been wet fen and mere, but also had to face the fact that in this time he had built up significant debts. Further problems arose with the collapse of wheat prices in the 1880s as cheaper imports from the North American grain fields began to find a ready market in Europe and at the time of William Wells' death in 1889, the sale of the estate to redeem outstanding debts was the only realistic option for his heirs. The catalogue drawn up for the sale of Holmewood and its estate emphasised the *"remarkably well drained, extremely fertile"* site of Whittlesea Mere, but also noted *"a large tract laid down to permanent pasture"*, indicating that arable cultivation was in retreat from the original vision for arable farming over the whole drained area. (32)

Indeed, the Foreword to the catalogue described the estate as *"a magnificent freehold residential and sporting domain"*, showing the growing significance of shooting rights on the estate, which at that time included 700 pheasant, as well as hare, partridge, wild fowl and *"rabbits by the thousand"*.

Maps from the latter part of the 19th century show how Holme Fen's raised bog was given over to cover for the birds whilst arable farming became increasingly confined to the mere bed as those fields not needed for pheasant cover were put down to permanent pasture. As the 1890 catalogue makes clear, whilst the mere bed farms, such as Black Ham and Engine and Lady Seat, were between 87% and 94% arable, by contrast, on those farms with significant peat land, such as Holme Lode Farm, the area of arable dropped as low as 68%.

An exception to this general picture in Holme parish, however, was Yaxley Fen, where arable remained the dominant land use, although this too was not without its problems, as farmers found wet spots, or *"bog holes"*, a treacherous hazard for horses and machinery alike:

> *"Another thing, the horses used to go down in the bog-hole. They used to lay down – so low. They just lay there until they're ready, then plunge out."*
>
> Walter Day, Fred Briggs (Interview, 24 February 1986)

As a result of these difficulties, as experienced in the 1920s, some of these fields were also allowed to revert to scrub and pasture:

*"Two or three fields down this roadside (Yaxley Road, Holme),
they was never cultivated much. They used to leave 'em – there was
a lot of bog-holes in them....the old horses couldn't walk across,
sink right down...big enough for two horses to drop through 'em."*

Ernie James (Interview, 13 June 1986)

Lord de Ramsey, who had purchased the estate in 1890, sold to J
Ashton Fielden in 1902. Fielden was a keen sportsman and a renowned
shot and it was his policy to manage the estate first and foremost for
its sporting value:

*"New Barn Farm, up until the last war [1939-1945] was nothing
but scrubland – bushes, bog – all but two fields which Mr Fielden
used to plough up and drill with corn every year and leave the
corn for his pheasants."*

Tim Mitcham (Interview 18 February 1986)

In spite of the problems associated with farming in the newly
drained peat fen, the years immediately following the drainage were
full of promise and yielded good crops which sustained the new
farms. The need for labour to work the land saw a major movement
of people onto the fen with new farms, their out-buildings and farm
cottages being built. The creation of the new civil parish of Holme in
1857, separating it for the first time from Glatton, acknowledged this
explosion of population living on the fen and the old mere bed.

The Reverend Broke, vicar of Holme, writing in 1897 noted:

*"In Holme Fen there are no fewer than 42 houses [in the fen], all
of which are over two miles, and many four, from their Parish
Church...[with] some 200 parishioners."*

Within a generation of the draining the Mere, the population living on
the fen exceeded the number of residents in the village of Holme itself.

The vicar's concern for the spiritual welfare of this farming population resulted in the unique provision of a floating church, a barge with cabin mounted on top of the hull and fitted out internally as a chapel. This was towed round the waterways of the parish to offer services at three regular stations at Charter Farm, Stokes Bridge and Allen's Engine. Several baptisms were conducted and the novelty and convenience of the mobile church ensured a steady attendance. (33)

The Fenland Ark, as it became known, operated for a period of seven and a half years before declining population, interest and the practical challenges of maintaining a regular schedule of services led to the provision being halted. The barge was then moved to Manea near Chatteris, on the Old Bedford River, where it again serviced isolated fen communities for a few more years.

Whilst a number of factors seem to have led to the mission of the Fenland Ark ending at Holme, it seems that already by the early years of the 20th century, the population in these isolated locations was declining, most likely as the acreage of pasture and woodland cover increased and the need for labourers to work the diminishing arable lands declined.

There nevertheless remained significant numbers of families, with children, on the fen throughout the latter decades of the 19th century and well into the 20th century. The journey to school was particularly difficult in the winter months and a dedication stone, mounted on the wall of the village school, records how Lady Louisa Wells, widow of William, endowed the school "bus service", first set up by her husband in 1877, to fetch the children from the fen farms and bring them in to school, and, of course, take them home again. The service was maintained into the 1920s when the waggon was driven by William Ayres, the local coal merchant. His son, Jim, described the waggon as a horse-drawn, four-wheeled trolley with hooped canvas top, fitted out with wooden seating along each side.

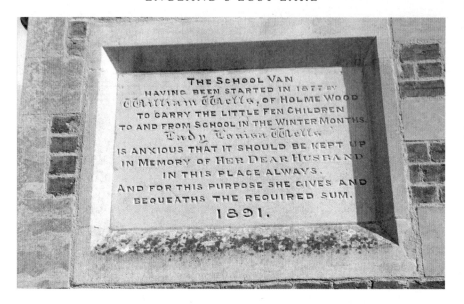

One incident with the van is described by Beattie Adams, whose family lived on Holme Lode Farm:

"I remember we was coming through that wood, nearly blew the van in the dyke, so we had to go in that farmhouse [Ladyseat]. Had to bring word round to parents and then dad had to piggy-back us over the dyke to get us home."

Beattie Adams (Interview 21 February 1986)

By the start of World War 2, although the old bed of Whittlesea Mere had remained under cultivation, much of the peatland, drained amid such a fanfare almost a hundred years before, had reverted to a mixture of pasture, scrub and woodland through a combination of intent and resignation at the reality of the unequal (and costly) struggle to make the land fit to yield good crops. Indeed, when Holme Fen was declared a national nature reserve in 1952, it was listed, not as fen at all, but as grade 1 woodland, and described as the finest example of birch wood in lowland Britain!

The World War, and the drive from the War Agricultural Committees to increase the supply of home grown produce began to turn things around, but the experience of the farmers shows that it was still an uphill struggle:

"New Barn Farm, up until the last war was nothing but scrubland – bushes, bog [apart from two fields sown with corn for Mr Fielden's pheasants]. Father had the job of more or less reclaiming it, but it still wasn't very good farmland. In fact it was terrible farmland. Tile drains were tried, but the peat is so deep and it moves around so much that the tile drains used to get out of line and become silted up in three or four years. It didn't become farmable until the advent of plastic drains which really transformed it."

Tim Mitcham (Interview 18 February 1986)

On Engine Farm, the experience was similar:

"We had 110 acres, specifically on the black – it was ragwort and short grass. It was just like a mown lawn because we had so many rabbits and the rabbits kept the grass well cropped...there came a time to plough it up – I think it was the War Ag at the time. It had 350 tons of clay an acre and it was my job when I left school to push this clay about with a Fordson Major tractor with a manually operated blade in front. I had six months pushing this stuff about, then we ploughed it in...it worked very well and it did make reasonable land of what was really one time just room out of doors."

John Bliss (Interview 27 May 1986)

J Ashton Fielden died in 1942 and the estate came into the ownership of the Crown Estates who continued the policy of improving the agricultural potential of the farms. The combination of improved drainage, improved farm machinery with in particular the advent of the tractor, and the mixing of large quantities of clay as described by John Bliss at Engine Farm or subsidised ground limestone dressing, as in the case of Lord's Farm, Yaxley Fen – all these, plus careful selection of crops to suit the varied soil conditions, resulted in the ploughing up of almost all the pasture fields, leaving the woodland of Holme Fen resting on what remained of the pre-drainage raised bog and preserving relict populations of a sample of the rich flora and fauna which had characterised the area before drainage. Field boundaries running through the wood remain as a reminder of the hopes of William Wells and his fellow drainers for broad acres of waving corn over the whole drained area of the 1850s. Whilst something of that vision had been achieved, this had only been made possible through constant upgrading of the drainage arrangements and regular investment in improving the soil condition for cropping.

By the 1980s the long recognised national importance of areas like Holme Fen and the nearby nature reserve at Woodwalton Fen was shown to be increasingly at risk as the efficiency of drainage inexorably dried out the fen deposits and threatened the survival of valuable wetland plant and insect species. New ideas were coming to the fore about the best use of this land and a vision was developed for a re-wilding of parts of the landscape, to provide for the conservation of the environment whilst still enabling some agricultural use and to provide an important educational and leisure resource for the local population. The Great Fen Project was born.

The Great Fen Project

What is the Great Fen?

In the 1990s it was recognised that the national nature reserves at Holme Fen and Woodwalton Fen were under threat from de-watering and were too small individually to support viable populations of the surviving important populations of flora and fauna. Following discussions involving a wide range of partners, the vision grew for the creation of a vast new wetland, protecting the existing reserves and linking the reserves with corridors for the movement of fauna and birds. The project was launched with the vision of restoring the area to a species rich wetland, beneficial to both local people and wildlife, over a 50 – 100 year period. In 2001 the Great Fen Partnership was formed and, with substantial funding from the Heritage Lottery Fund, land extending over 3700 hectares (9143 acres) was acquired and the process of reshaping the landscape got underway.

The Great Fen is one of the largest restoration projects of its type in Europe.

What is happening with Whittlesea Mere now?

The Mere itself cannot be recreated as the great body of water which once existed, but the former site of the Mere is being transformed

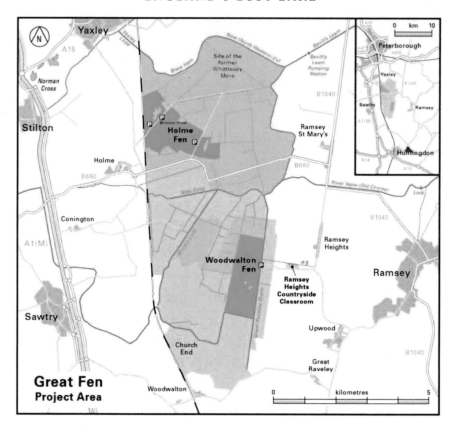

into a mosaic of different habitats. Land which has been under arable cultivation since the mid 19th century is gradually being changed into grassland for stock rearing and, in parts, to wet meadow, where stock can still be seasonally grazed.

A dynamic, changing landscape is evolving, with the creation of meres, wildflower meadows, new linear pools, and reed beds in order to encourage and support a rich diversity of wildlife, some not seen since the drainage of the meres in the 19th century. With the re-profiling of existing ditches, and the digging of new dykes, water is now conserved within the area, rather than draining it away as quickly as possible.

The Holme Fen Posts: original post furthest, scale one metre.
When erected, c 1852, ground surface was on the level of the top of the posts

A 10 km (c 6 mile) circular walk called "The Last of the Meres" and a 3.5 km (c 2 mile) "Northern Loop" extension walk are open to the public, bringing together fascinating heritage and a wealth of wildlife for people to discover and enjoy.

The Future of the Great Fen

Regular monitoring of water levels, monthly species counts of birdlife and mammals, and coordinated spot observations across the fen enable our understanding of the developing landscape to grow, allowing adjustments in planning. Already significant successes have been recorded, such as the return of populations of bittern, snipe and jack snipe and the remarkable spread of aquatic plant species, dragonflies, damsel flies and moths as new habitats are established.

Places to walk, cycle and ride horses are being developed continuously and a visitor centre and café are planned. The future of the Great Fen is one that will create a sustainable environment, support local businesses and provide people with a place to really enjoy wildlife, heritage and the great outdoors.

For more information, see www.greatfen.org.uk.

What to see?

THE HOLME FEN POST (TL 204895)

William Wells erected an iron post, said to have been brought from the Great Exhibition of 1851, to act as a gauge by which to measure the land subsidence following drainage of the Mere. This was not the first post to be erected in the fen, but succeeded one of three timber piles put up some years before. The surface level in 1848 was recorded as 5 feet 7 inches (1 .74m) O.D. It is a remarkable fact that the present (1986) land surface is some 13 feet (4m) lower, that is 7 feet 5 inches below sea level.

Since 1957 there have been two Holme Fen posts, because the original was found to be unstable. A new post was erected to ensure the continuing accurate measurement of the land subsidence. An information board at the site illustrates how the original post was fixed to the clay bed underlying the peat – a remarkable feat in itself.

HOLME FEN NATIONAL NATURE RESERVE

The reserve has a number of open access footpaths through the woodland and leading to the meres, created by the Nature Conservancy in the 1980s. Since then the Great Fen Project has been developing a network of public footpaths and there is now a route through the woods to Rymes Reedbed, where water scrapes and small meres have been created to encourage wildfowl. A superb bird hide is open at all times.

Much of the reserve is, in fact , Grade 1 woodland, predominantly birch, rather than fen, but there are some important areas of former wetland vegetation cover, including the rare fen woodrush around the meres and in open clearings.

WOODWALTON FEN NATIONAL NATURE RESERVE

Like Holme Fen, since the advent of the Great Fen Project, Woodwalton Fen is now open access. Woodwalton is more typical of the pre-drainage fenland than is Holme Fen, with fine stretches of reed bed, fen carr and open meres. This was the location for efforts to reintroduce the continental Large Copper Butterfly and is now the home of the fen violet, a rare survivor in modern fenland and where in 2016, the bittern successfully bred again..

MERE BED

After ploughing, the lake bed of Trundle Mere is visible as a lighter soil contrasting with the black peats of the reed shoals and surrounding peatland. This is best seen from the public footpath running along the banks of Yaxley Lode/Black Ham River. With the re-wilding of the farm fields which were laid out over the former sites of Whittlesea Mere and Dray Mere, the lighter coloured marl soils of the mere beds are now covered with vegetation.

ENGINE FARM STONES (TL 233903)

When Whittlesea Mere was drained 17 stone blocks were recovered. They had presumably been on their way from the quarries at Barnack to Ramsey Abbey, being carried on a barge that overturned. Four of the blocks can still be seen at Engine Farm today. Access during normal working hours during the week.

JOHNSON'S POINT PUMPING STATION (TL 237904)

Sadly, the original pumping station, housing the centrifugal pump seen at the Great Exhibition, has been demolished, although the housings for its diesel and electric powered successors can be seen by following the Last of the Meres Trail, as well as the Engineer's house. The original impeller from Appold's pump and the scale model exhibited in 1851 can be seen at the Science Museum in London.

THE CENSER AND INCENSE BOAT

The censer, complete with chain, stands eleven inches high on a circular foot. Made of silver gilt, it is thought to be of English workmanship, of the mid 14th century. The incense boat, also in silver gilt, is eleven inches long and stands three inches high on a hexagonal foot. It is decorated with the rams' heads, indicative of Ramsey Abbey ownership, and an early (end of 15th century) double Tudor rose. Both pieces are now in the Victoria and Albert Museum, London.

THE LAST OF THE MERES TRAIL

The Last of the Meres trail is a circular walk connecting the northern parts of the Great Fen. It extends from restored areas at New Decoy Farm to the historic site of Engine Farm, through to the woodland of Holme Fen and back via the old Holme-to-Ramsey railway line. The route crosses the former site of Whittlesea Mere.

FENLAND ARK

Nothing now remains of the vessel itself but the lectern (reading desk) from the water-borne chapel still survives and can be seen in St Mary Magdalene Church in Stilton. The churchyard too has an interesting feature linked to the history of the Whittlesea Mere in the tombstone of John Bodger, the surveyor responsible for the silk map (see centre spread).

References

FNQ   Fenland Notes and Queries
HRO   Huntingdon Record Office
ILN   Illustrated London News
VCH   Victoria County History

I.   This is probably a 12th century fabrication as it stands, although there may still be some truth in its assertions. The pre-Domesday antiquity of Whittlesea Mere itself need not be doubted for it also receives mention in Thorney charters of the late l0th century: A.J. Robertson Anglo Saxon Charters Cambridge 1939, p.253.

2.   W.T. Bree Recollections of a morning's ramble ... Phytologist 4 1851, p.98-105.

3.   Natural History letters, 25 March 1825. We owe this reference to R.Lines.

4.   The Reverend Nowers' letter concerning the acorn is published in J.M.Heathcote Reminiscences of fen and mere London 1876, p.82-83. John Shelton: 1851 Census, Yaxley , s. v.; Bree (op. cit.) refers to a collector and dealer in Yaxley in 1848.

5.   Hunts. Post, 7 April 1906.

6.   State Papers dom. 16/230 f. 50 (A.D. 1637) For more background to this event and its aftermath, see K. Lindley Fen and Riots and the English Revolution London 1982, p.94-95. The document is quoted in FNQ 5 (1901-1903), p.363.

7.   S. Inskipp Ladds mss. Holme (notes preparatory to writing the V.C.H.) held by the Norris Museum, St. Ives.

8.   H.C. Darby Medieval Fenland Newton Abbot 1974, p.14, n.5.

9.   W.H. Hart, P.A. Lyons, edd. Cartularium Monasterii de Rameseia II, p.364-366.

10. H.R. 0 . 106 Box dd F5, Bundle 49.

11. Inskipp Ladds op.cit. n.7.

12. FNQ II (1894) p.320-322.

13. FNQ II (1894) p.l33-134.

14. Peterborough Advertiser, 23 April 1887.

15. This account of the wildfowling and reed cutting draws substantially on an article which appeared in the Peterborough Advertiser (II February 1905) augmented by the unpublished memories of Mr. T. Blackman of Yaxley (1911), and oral evidence from surviving members of the Coles' family.
The story of John Beharral appears several times with minor variations, but the earliest published account is by Edward Bradley, who published under the alias Cuthbert Bede in Leisure Hour 1877, p.296-300.
16. ILN 19 January 1850.
17. Letter of Thomas Rooper dated 12 November 1864 (H.R.O. Con 8/ 3.)
18. F. Buller Domesday Book of Mammoth Pike 1979. p.214.
19. FNQ I (1889-1891), p.230, quoting a newspaper cutting of 9 June 1840.
20. FNQ II (1894) p.39.
21. Recorded' by Rooper (op.cit. n.l7)
22. J .W. Childers ed. Lord Orford's Voyage around the Fens in 1774 Doncaster 1868. See also for helpful commentary, F.H. Stallard Lord Orford's Voyage 1974 (Typescript held by Peterborough Central Library, Local Studies Collection).
23. H. R. 0. HMC/73, F 49/31 .
24. ILN 19 January 1850.
25. Heathcote op.cit. n.4, p.36-37.
26. H.R. 0. 106 Box dd F4, Bundle 6. Piecemeal reclamation around the edge of the Mere had already begun by c. 1810: R. Parkinson General View of the Agricultural . . Huntingdon 1811, p.l9.
27. H.R.O. Box dd F5, Bundle 6.
28. ILN 22 November 1851.
29. Peterborough Advertiser. II February 1905. Both the censer and incense boat are now (1986) at the Victoria and Albert Museum.
30. W. Wells 'The Drainage of Whittlesea Mere' Journal of the Royal Agricultural Society 21 (1860), p. l34-153 .
31. ILN 26 April 1851.
32 Holmewood Estate Sale Particulars, 23 July 1890 HRO 5345/3/1
33 J Bennett The Fenland Ark 1983

Appendix A

Notes on the Flora of the Whittlesea Mere area

Drawing on a number of sources, we can build up an extensive list of the species collected and identified in the Huntingdonshire fens around Whittlesea Mere before its drainage. The number of uncommon, rare and very rare species represented highlights the extraordinary botanical interest and value of this wetland landscape. Consideration of the species still present on the two major reserves in the area , Holme Fen and Woodwalton Fen, whilst indicating their present significance, also shows just how much has been lost.

Naturalists' journals, in particular those of the Marchioness of Huntly, who lived at Orton Longueville Hall and visited the fens around the Mere regularly, both before and after drainage , help us to chart the gradual drying out of the peat land and the progress of cultivation, which together combined to squeeze out many plants from their last remaining refuges by the end of the 19th century.

One of the most vulnerable habitats was, of course, the raised acid bog. The Sphagnum moss has survived at Holme Fen, but the flowering plants which colonised the moss have all vanished – bog rosemary, bog orchid, mountain everlasting and the cranberry – and other species characteristic of the acid bog, have likewise become extinct in the locality – cotton grass, common butterwort, marsh cinquefoil and marsh voilet. The surviving flora gives a vital clue to the former habitat but cannot match its richness either in scale or variety.

We have appended a selected list of species noted in the 19th century, omitting many more common species which are less indicative of the particular conditions in the Whittlesea Mere area .

Source list:

J Sheail, TCE Wells *The Marchioness of Huntly: the written record and the Herbarium*, **Biological Journal of the Linnean Society 13 (1980), p.315-330**

GC Druce, *Botany*, **VCH Huntingdonshire I p.29-80**

SPECIES	STATUS in G.B.	HABITAT	PRESENT Holme Fen (HF) Woodwalton Fen (WF)
Anagallis ten. (bog pimpernel)	Uncommon	Peat bog amongst moss	WF
Andromeda polo (bog rosemary)	Rare	In Sphagnum moss	Lost
Antennaria diocia (mountain everlasting)	Uncommon	In Sphagnum moss	Lost
Baldelia ran. (lesser w ater plantain)	Very rare in South Britain	In peaty dykes	
Blechnum spi. (common hand fern)	-	Damp acid heath	Lost
Calluna vulg. (heather)	-	Acid conditions	
Carex pul. (flea sedge)	-	Calcarous fen	
Cirsium dis. (meadow thistle)	Uncommon	Damp, peaty marshes	
Cladium mar. (great fen sedge)	Uncommon	Fens	
Dacty. incarnata (early marsh orchid)	Uncommon	Damp, peaty grassland	
Drosera anglica (great sundew)			Lost
intermed. (oblong leaved s.)	Uncommon	Peat bog	Lost
Rotund. (common sundew)			Lost
Dryopteris crist. (crested buckler fern)	Very rare	Only on boggy heaths	Lost
dilitata (broad buckler fen)	–	Heaths, damp acid soils	HF, WF
carthus. (narrow buckler fen)	Uncommon	Bogs	HF, WF
Epipactus pal. (marsh hellebore)	Uncommon	Peat bog	Lost
Eric tetralix (cross leaved heath)	-	Peat bog	HF, WF
Eriophorium ang. (common cottongrass)	-	Acid bog	Lost
Galium sax. (heathbedstraw)	-	Heathy places	Lost
Hammarbya palud. (bog orchid)	-	Acid places or Sphagnum moss	Lost
Molinia cae. (purple moor grass)	-	Acid soils, fens	HF, WF
Myrica gale (bog myrtle)	Uncommon	Wet heaths	HF, WF
Narthecium oss. (bog asphodel)	Uncommon	Wet heaths	Lost
Parnessia pal. (grass of Parnassus)	Uncommon	Marshy places	Lost

SPECIES	STATUS in G.B.	HABITAT	PRESENT Holme Fen (HF) Woodwalton Fen (WF)
Pedicularis pal. (marsh lousew ort)	Uncommon	Wet heaths	Lost
Peucedanum pal. (milk parsley)	Rare	Fens, marshes	Lost
Pinguicula vulg. (common butterw ort)	-	Acid bog	Lost
Polystichum set. (soft shield fern)	Uncommon	Wet places	Lost
Potentilla pal. (marsh cinquefoil)	-	Acid bog	Lost
Pteridium aquil. (bracken)	-	-	HF, WF
Rumex hyd. (w ater dock)	-	Wet places	HF, WF
Salix repens (creeping w illow)	-	Bogs	HF, WF
Samolus val. (brookw eed)	Uncommon	Damp places	HF, WF
Schoenus nig. (black bog rush)	Uncommon	Peaty areas	Lost
Scutellaria gader. (skullcap)	-	By fresh water	HF, WF
Senecio pal. (marsh fleaw ort)	Extinct	Marshes	Lost
pallud. (fen ragw ort)	Very rare	Fens	Lost
aqu. (marsh ragw ort)	–	Damp grassland	Lost
Eru. (hoary ragw ort)	Uncommon	Damp grassland	HF, WF
Stellaria pal. (marsh stitchw ort)	Rare	Wet grassy places	WF
Thalictrum f lav.	Uncommon	Wet grassy places Acid soils	HF, WF
Thelypteris lim. (lemon scented fern)	Uncommon	Wet places among Sundew , heathers And asphodels	Lost
Pal. (marsh fern)	Uncommon	Wet places among Sundew , heathers And asphodels	Lost
Utriclaria mon. (lesser bladderw ort)	Uncommon	In shallow water	Lost
Vulg. (greater bladderw ort)	Uncommon	In water	WF
Vaccinium oxy. (cranberry)	Rare	Sphagnum bogs	Lost
Valeriana dioca (marsh valerian)	Uncommon	Marshy fields	Lost
Viola pal. (marsh violet)	–	Acid bog	Lost
Pers. (fen violet)	Very rare	Alkaline fen in long grass	WF
Wahlenbergia hed, (ivy leaved bellflower)	Rare	Damp heath	Lost

Senecio Paludosus ~ extinct.

Appendix B:

Butterflies & Moths

There follows a list of species closely associated with the Mere and the raised bog at Holme Fen. In 1986, only four of the moths still survive in the area. The historical notes make clear how collectors focussed their attention on the Huntingdonshire fens in the early 19th century and revealed the richness and importance of these wetlands as a particular habitat supporting a range of rare insects.

The drainage of the Mere and its associated works are often assumed to have been the primary cause of the extinction of many of these creatures. But the table also shows that , in fact, very few of the key food plants, on which the butterflies and moths depended, became extinct as a result of drainage. To take an example, Phragmites (common reed) remained a significant crop in the area into the 20th century with reed beds in the fen at Woodwalton and Conington and, in addition, crops of dyke reeds were taken and laid in farmyards and droves on Whittlesea Mere up until 1920 at least. Yet only the Brown Veined Wainscot Moth , out of three species associated with Phragmites (s.v. Nos 8-10) has survived to the present day.

The continuous and general drying out of the fens under various drainage schemes led to an increasing interest being focussed on the Whittlesea Mere area in the early 19th century as one of the few remaining wetland habitats. As a result, the pressure of collectors on already dwindling insect populations became severe. The impact on particular species is obvious enough (s.v. No.6 Whittlesea Satin Moth), but the effect was also spread much wider by the employment of local labourers , who collected heavily and at random:

"about sixteen additional examples (of a beetle, Trechus Incitis) have been captured in the fens between Holme and Yaxley, Huntingdonshire, by a labouring man employed by the late Mr. Jarman to collect insects for him, and who sent those to him among a vast mass of useless things ." (4)

It seems, therefore, that a declining habitat combined with the pressure of collectors led to the destruction of many of these species.

Sources

1. J. Balding "Lepidoptera" in S.H. Miller, S.B.J. Skertchley The Fen/and 1878, p.40l-412.
2. R. South Moths of the British Isles 1907.
3. W.T. Bree "Recollections of a morning's ramble in the Whittlesea Fens" Phytologist 4 (1851) p.98-l05.
4. J.F. Dawson "Coleoptera. Notes on British Geodophaga" Entomologists Annual 2 (1856) p.65-8l.

SPECIES	Date first recorded	Date last recorded	Food Plant	Food plant Present (P) or last recorded
1. Swallow Tail Butterfly	abundant in 1829	Before 1978	milk parsley	1845
2. Large Copper Butterfly	1795	1847/8	great water dock	P
3. Reed Leopard Moth	1841	Before 1878	common reed	P
4. Scarlet Tiger Moth	?	Before 1878	nettle, groundsel, bramble, sloe sallow, comfrey	P
5. Gypsy Moth	1828	1842-1850	oak, elm, sallow, hawthorn, sloe	P
6. Reed Tussock or Whittlesea Ermine or Whittlesea Satin Moth	1819/20	c.1871	burr reed, great fen, sedge, common read	P
7. Marsh Carpet Moth	1848	Present	common meadow rue	?
8. Reed Dagger Moth	?	Before 1878	common reed	P

SPECIES	Date first recorded	Date last recorded	Food Plant	Food plant Present (P) or last recorded
9. Flame Wainscot Moth	?	?	common reed	P
10. Brown veined Wainscot	?	Present	common reed	P
11. Haworth's Minor Moth	1829	Before 1878	cotton grass	1850
12. Silver Barred Moth	?	1850?	purple moor grass, smooth meadow grass	P
13. Concobrous Moth	1844	Present	wood small-reed	P
14. Mere Wainscot Moth	1847	Present	purple small-reed wood small	P
15. Rosy Marsh Moth	1837	1851?	bog myrtle, sallow	P
16. Beautiful Yellow Underwing Moth	?	?	ling, heather	P

Additional Notes to Species List (Appendix B)

Figures in brackets refer to numbered sources, 1-4.

1. No notices have been received of recent captures at Whittlesea Mere, Holme Fen, Yaxley Fen and localities. (1)

2. Formerly in abundance at Whittlesea Mere and Holme Fen. (1) *"The splendid Lycaena Dispar, one while captured here abundantly, is now, I am told, scarcely if at all, to be found in the locality. Its existence in Britain will probably ere long be a matter of history – one of the things which were and are not. A collector and dealer at Yaxley informed me in the summer of 1848, that he had that season most diligently searched up and down all the dykes , and could scarcely find a single caterpillar; and he had, I think, only one specimen of the butterfly in his boxes"*. (3) A continental sub-species introduced at Woodwalton Fen in the 1980s failed to become established.

3. Formerly abundant at Holme Fen, Yaxley Fen and Whittlesea Mere, where it was first discovered by Mr. Doubleday. (1) The earliest known British locality for the species was Holme Fen in Huntingdonshire (1841-1848). In 1850 it was found abundantly at Whittlesea Mere. (2)

4. Formerly abundant at Whittlesea Mere (1).. . about 1850 it had almost, or quite ceased to exist, as a wilding, in England. Stephens ... writing in 1828, states that at that time it abounded in the Huntingdonshire Fens. (2)

6. It was formerly abundant at Whittlesea Mere, having first been discovered on the Yaxley portion of the Mere in 1820 by Mr. Standish.(1) The insect was formerly abundant in some parts of fen land , and was first met with, as a British species, at Whittlesea Mere about 1819 or 1820 ... by 1865 larvae at a shilling per dozen, the price at which they had been sold by the reed cutters, were no longer obtainable, and they became so scarce that in the year 1871 or thereabouts, only two caterpillars were seen. (2) *"The Whittlesea satin moth too , I was told, used to be found in certain parts of the fens, but has not been met with of late years".* (3)

7. ... it was not known as British until 1848, when Mr. Doubleday received a specimen from the Old Whittlesea Mere locality. (I) Doubleday recorded it as British in the Zoologist for 1848. He there states: *"A single example of this pretty species was obtained last season near Peterborough but I believe it was not in very good condition. A splendid female was sent to me from the same neighbourhood this week"* (15 July 1848). (2) This species is still present at both Holme Fen and Woodwalton Fen in 1986.

10. First taken in 1846 at Whittlesea Mere by Mr. Shepherd. (I) ... until 1900 it had not been noted in England for a number of years, and specimens were only known from Yaxley and Whittlesea . (2) This species is still present at both Holme Fen and Woodwalton Fen in 1986.

11. Taken formerly at Whittlesea Mere in great plenty, which was the only locality given by Stephens, Wood and other early writers. (I) It was first noticed as British in 1819, and Stephens in 1829 mentions it as common in Whittlesea Mere. (2)

12. Formerly near Whittlesea Mere. With the destruction of Whittlesea Mere, this species was believed to have become extinct in the district. (I) In ancient times it occurred in Norfolk and at Whittlesea Mere. (2)

13. This species was at one time found subsequent to 1844, when it was first discovered in Yaxley Fen, not at all scarce in that locality . ... it then disappeared from all its old haunts, some of which were destroyed . (2) This species is still present at both Holme Fen and Woodwalton Fen in 1986.

14. Formerly Yaxley, where it was first taken in 1847, used to be a noted locality, but the insect disappeared when the fen was drained. (2)   This species is still present at both Holme Fen and Woodwalton Fen in 1986.

15. This handsome moth was discovered by Weaver about 1837 at Yaxley Fen in Huntingdonshire. According to Barrett, Doubleday in 1846 sent English to collect some and he found it plentiful at both Yaxley and Whittlesea Mere. No further mention has been made of it and when the fens were drained about 1851 it is presumed to have become extinct. (2)

Further Reading

Many of these volumes are now out of print, but for the interested reader, they will be found in local history libraries and county record offices.

A.K. ASTBURY
The Black Fens
Ely 1987
A good general introduction to the peat fenland.

J BENNETT
The Fenland Ark
Mapro Publishing 1983
The fascinating story of the floating mission church which served the farming families who settled on the drained fen around Whittlesea Mere.

J.W. CHILDERS ed.
Lord Orford's Voyage round the Fens in 1774
British Library 2011
Entertaining diary account of the eccentric Lord Orford's adventures sailing round the fens before the meres were drained.

J COLES & D HALL
Changing Landscapes: the Ancient Fenland
Wetland Archaeological Research Group 1998
The best short summary considering the archaeology of the fenland basin which draws extensively on David Hall's legendary fieldwalking programme in the peat fens and the more detailed volumes of the Fenland Survey.

T COOK, REM PILCHER
History of Borough Fen Decoy
Providence Press 1982
An informative record of the practice of catching birds by the ancient art of the decoy, which was brought to the fens in the 17th century. Gives an insight into the importance of this source of food in the past. As Whittlesea Mere declined as a body of water, the Holme Fen decoy was created, its location echoed now in the farm names of Old Decoy and New Decoy off the Ramsey road.

H.C. DARBY
Medieval England
Newton Abbot 1974
The classic study which has not been replaced as an excellent starting point for understanding the richness of the fen in medieval times.

H.C. DARBY
The Changing Fenland
Cambridge 1983
Tells the story of the developing drainage of the fens from medieval times up to the 20th century. An excellent and well illustrated introduction.

H. GODWIN
Fenland: Its Ancient Past and Uncertain Future
Cambridge 1978
Focusses more on the ecology of the fens and a good companion volume to Darby 1983 for obtaining a rounded picture of developments over time and appreciating the unique character of the peat fenland.

J.M. HEATHCOTE
Reminiscences of Fen and Mere
London 1876
An entertaining account of the Whittlesea Mere area by an eye-witness to and participant in the 19th century shooting parties and other social activities which were such a feature of the latter part of Whittlesea Mere's life.

J.M. HUTCHINSON
The record of peat wastage at Holme Fen 1848-1978 A.D.
Journal of Ecology 68 (1980)
p. 229-249

S OOSHUIZEN
The Anglo-Saxon Fenland
Windgather Press 2017
An up to date and thoroughly researched short book which focusses strongly on the management of fen resources.

I.D. ROTHERAM
The Lost Fens: England's greatest ecological disaster 2013
The clue is in the title.

E STOREY
Spirit of the Fens Hale 1985
A local writer (his poetry is also well worth exploring) with a great heart for the fen and its people. Light of touch, full of anecdote and humour.

VICTORIA COUNTY HISTORY, Huntingdonshire volume III
Essential background information on local parishes and aspects of general history, economic, social etc.

W WELLS

The drainage of Whittlesea Mere

Journal of the Royal Agricultural Society 21 (1860) p.134-153

The classic account by the man primarily responsible for the drainage of the Mere. Worth digging out to get a feel for the optimism of the age of improvement.

Stewart Howe, Chair of the Fenland Trust, sponsors of the publication with the author outside the Admiral Wells, the lowest pub in the British Isles.